LEMON HOUND

LEMON HOUND

SINA QUEYRAS

COACH HOUSE BOOKS | TORONTO

Published with the assistance of the Canada Council for
the Arts and the Ontario Arts Council. We also acknowl-
edge the financial support of the Government of Ontario
through the Ontario Book Publishing Tax Credit Program
and the Government of Canada through the Book
Publishing Industry Development Program.

LIBRARY AND ARCHIVES CANADA
CATALOGUING IN PUBLICATION

Queyras, Sina, 1963-
    Lemon hound / Sina Queyras. -- 1st ed.

Poems.
ISBN-13: 978-1-55245-167-0
ISBN-10: 1-55245-167-4

    I. Title.

PS8583.U3414L44 2006   C811'.6   C2006-901135-4

'As for the *mot juste*, you are quite wrong. Style is a very simple matter; it is all rhythm. Once you get that, you can't use the wrong words.'

Virginia Woolf

TABLE OF CONTENTS

Lake of the Woods, August 1993

Loons Virginia. Open sky. Waves of trees. Dizzying trees. Pine and balsam: a billion party picks. Roads shoot off, paved, unpaved, trail, tundra, trapline, blue lines of rivers and lakes all the way to the Hudson Bay. She scans possible routes while you change shoes, prepare to hike up Asheham Hill with Pinker. Freezing and unfreezing. Trees shrinking. Even the shape of the lakes appears frozen. Red pine, white pine: tall with uneven branches of varying lengths. Slightly taller with uneven branches of varying lengths. Pipe cleaners, deeper and deeper green. Lake and lake and lake: Deer, Poplar Hill, North Spirit, Wunnumin, Summer Beaver, Miró-like in muskeg. And rivers: Severn, Fawn, Pipestone, Asheweig: their magnet pull north. She grips the wheel, chain-smoking from Clayoquot through the west's fuming neon huddles. Macadam miles, navigation of geographic land mines. Lakeless, loonless, somehow Canadian and mute to all this: red pine, white pine, black spruce, black ash, trembling aspen, balsam fir, white birch, white spruce, but which is which? Balsam poplar, tamarack – they all look the same from the window. Jack pines feed on fire, she reads, and wonders if this is all second growth. Has this whole land been mowed? Are these forest fringes? Tender scars hidden for drive-by viewing: *big trees ... scarce as whales.* A campground beckons. She surfaces, inflates the tent, the dog marking all four corners before they walk to the dark pine lake, crouch on the Canadian Shield and stare at their reflection. She leans close and a rush of pine penetrates. She will enter into, finally tongue this idea of who she is. A thunder of feet upends, her whole head submerges, eyes open in the green and black pine water. Atwood Lake: it has leapt up, throttled her, left her an X in the landscape. Stare and stare, as a loon circles, dives, pregnant with itself: flap and flap, black and white, every ounce of its white-banded neck muscling. Stand and shake, the desert of her lungs wanting to turn herself inside out. The loon calls. Tremulous, it taps into her spine. It calls again. Her chest vibrates with it: a sad Icelander drunk with sagas, lost on a waveless lake in northern Manitoba, yodelling into the night, a rogue alarm clock *ha-ha-hoo-oo-oo*ing. It is cold where she is going, Virginia, though she cannot imagine how cold just yet, nor how far she will go; at this moment she still believes things occur in increments. Partial. She sees your pale feet at the water's edge and suddenly the rocks are scalloped, the trees manicured. Is this altogether too much nature for you? You who entered it so completely? You pull a cigarette out and she offers you a light. You sit smoking. All night the loon calls, but you are both silent. You are both so polite, waiting.

A RIVER BY THE MOMENT

'What is nature.
Nature is what is …
but is nature natural.
No not as natural as that.'

Gertrude Stein

The river is all thumbs

She is feeling brisk at the heel. She loves feeling brisk at the heel. She is feeling brisk at the heel and rivering her thumbs. She is at the edge of cool. She runs her thumbs along the hinge of river. She loves running her thumbs along the hinge of river. She feels river. She feels thumb. She is brisk and thumbing. She is numb and loving. She is feeling loving. She is feeling loving about feeling. She loves feeling about loving. She loves feeling about feeling. She loves feeling about feeling loving. Her loving feels. Her loving loves rivers. She is feeling loving about rivers. She loves feeling loving about rivers. She is feeling rivers about loving feeling. She rivers about loving. She rivers about feeling. She rivers about the hinges of rivers. Her feelings hinge. She hinges about feelings. She hinges about feeling the river of hinges. She is feeling thumbs. She loves feeling about her thumbs. She is feeling about her thumbs as she rivers her feelings. Her thumbs river. Her feelings cool. She feels cool rivering her thumbs. She feels her thumbs hinge the river and cooling she thumbs. She loves feeling that her thumbs hinge the river. She thumbs numb love.

Numb is more natural

Who is more numb? Who feels more numb about love? Who thumbs love? Who is numb about thumbing love? Who is more brisk, more river than hinge? Who is under water? Who loves being under water? Who is feeling swift and hinging under water, thumbless and numb in love? Who has wings? Who is mourning? Who is exactly how small they must be? Who is loss of action? Who has walked the Brooklyn Bridge? Who is turning forty and hingeless? Who is turning fifty and numb? Who is willing to bear? Who sees themselves a river? Who floats? Who eddies? Whose back is scraped? Whose knees bleed? Whose breasts ache? Who has a mouthful of water? Who knows the shape of rocks? Who sees the sun as wavelength? Who smells like trout? Whose spine flexes waterfalls? Who has been sixteen? Who is molten? Who is smoothed over? Who has not forgiven? Who has wet feet? Who has walked the river? Who has good drainage? Who has stubbed a toe on a rock? Who has felt granite on tooth? Who has seen the flash of red bellies? Who has eaten trout? Who has felt a bear paw? Who flirts with the snouts of wolves? Who is always fresh? Who is surface and depth? Who has walked the turnpike? Who is exactly how big they must be? Who has snagged the comma of mouth? Who understands trespassing? Who has not felt the earth under foot? Who knows the river bottom? Who of us is not hooked?

Even the idea of river

The river flows through the town. The river flows through the town and breaks up at the bridge. The river flows through the town slowly. The river is the fastest thing in town. The river is not confined to town. The river is townless, yet the river is town, for without the river there is no town. Without the river there are no riverbanks. Without the river there is no mill. Without the river there are no bridges. Without the river roads go on. Without the river foundations crack. Without the river fishermen turn to drink. Without the river old women cannot cry. Without the river no one is married. Without the river fossils soar. Without the river emerald and sage. Without the river lyrics are homeless. Without the river June never comes. Without the river mirrorless, the sky mourns. Without the river deer go deaf. Without the river leaves thirst. Without the river bear lose their teeth. Without the river beak, paw, soil, feather. Without the river the mountains shy. Without the river the ducks pass in the air, days climb one on another. Without the river children cannot learn how to count. Without the river there are no wings. Without the river nothing passes. Without the river stillness. Without the river trees turn away. Without the river the sun is angry. Without the river the land is seamless. Without the river it breaks apart. Without the river fish walk. Without the river rocks scurry. Without the river the town pulls up its skirt. Without the river bear and cougar nod into the earth's elbow, sleep.

What the river wants

The river wants the town to hug her but the town has an odour. The river wants to love the odour but it can't. The river wants the town to know this. The river wants the town to be invited. The river wants the town to paint itself red. The river wants the town to understand it. The river wants the town to talk softly. The river wants the town to step inside. The river wants the town to get over itself. The river wants the town to make way. The river wants the town to hug her without odour. The river wants the town to let her hug it too. The river wants to flood the town with anger. The river wants to fill its basements and cellars. The river wants to dig up graves and twirl them down Main Street. The river wants to flush out pantries and libraries. The river wants to lap her way through schools and courtrooms. The river wants to swallow the town the way it swallows her. The river wants the last gulp.

With or without rivets

She can name a thousand corporate logos. Her hands and feet are not easily disassembled. She knows fear. She understands Internet wallpaper, Happy Meals and smart bombs. She doesn't worry about cyborg subjectivity. She is a fully unlicenced florist. She is a hothouse. She has seen a thousand Gertrude Steins each more diluted. She plants seeds where she lingers. She is ontological. She is not simian. She is not leaf. She is not green. She no longer smells of the forest. She knows Jeanne d'Arc is dead. She knows the names of trees. She cares nothing for virginal. She worries about water. She stokes rage. She is more engine than mother. She has touched bullet holes. She has no walls. She drinks seaweed. She thinks uranium and glasses shatter. She fears corporate convicts. She remembers Janis. She has not yet sinned enough. She loves that her hands and feet are not easily disassembled. She is free to sniff out and string up. She understands facial reconstructions. She considers surgery. She has Emma's night vision. She is not without dog. She is scented. She is tie-dyed. She dreams of wings and glass shatters. She is historical and senseless. She is not without God. She is sensual. She has seeds under her tongue. She hopes for corporate convictions. She is no longer leaf. She is ontological jelly. She hears Sappho. She files her index finger. She has morphed. She feels the town pinching her shoulder blades. She cannot say that if she were the river she would allow the town to hug her. She feels for the sky. She holds the goddess by the toenails. She cannot swallow. She does not know. She has licked nothing. She has earned much. She ponders Emily.

Not leaf, nothing to green about

We have swallowed our god. We have manicured our toes. We live in apartments of plaster and steel. We have spliced our potato. We drive on roads named for the trees we cut to build them and the birds we displace with them and the towns we have left to come to them. We drive on steel cable. We pass by. We litter. We spew. We key in. We gambol in enclosed spaces. We commune with technology incessantly. We give up parts of ourselves. We pay tolls. We funnel and are funnelled. We are photographed and scanned. We fear men with specific accents. We subject ourselves. We think in pockets. We have sashes. We live in Iqaluit. We condescend. We give up freedom for the illusion of security. We know that John Wayne is dead. We shrink. We want to believe. We want to give. We buy flowers. We love our saddle-bags. We love our corrals. We don't understand our food. We live in L.A. We admire. We click. We spend hours online. We have call waiting. We send and receive. We envision wired houses of straw. We dream of solar panels, open air on clean land. We still believe in cowboys and teepees. We know about organic. We understand the structure of screen-plays. We baste babies who bear symphonic resemblances to historical figures. We are fully functioning. We scale coffee shops. We are radioactive. We make choices. We are live-wired. We try to forget the garden. We build buildings. We know that John Lennon is dead. We comb our hair. We fear spiders.

We defibrillate. We are orange. We squat and side kick simultaneously. We embrace contained soil. We design spaces. We save coupons. We think in scenes. We carry toxins in our fat. We give birth. We drive hybrids. We no longer think of the old days. We spend hours waiting for tech support. We are automated. We have forgotten more than we've read. We fold the new into our ovaries. We are implanted, impregnated, sterile. We want our childbirthing to be surgical. We are ruby. We calmly repeat information. We understand how to make ourselves heard. We gather. We deliver babies. We are ironic. We embrace perversity. We walk across rivers. We have legs like nutcrackers. Our hearts run out of batteries. We call 911. We live in New York. We know that JFK is dead. We collect coupons. We walk across bridges. We know how to shoot. We live in Toronto. We can tell time by the TV schedule. We know when to click. We recall traces of garden. We live in wired houses. We are plugged in but we are disconnected. We are girded. We know that John Donne is dead. We carry on. We skewer. We fracture. We wave in passing. We wait expectantly for commercials. We taste the Arctic in tomatoes. We should feel. We know a good mousse when we eat one.

Whose genealogy?

To claim genealogy, to bear the burden of, to be stepped on, dug up and dumped in, to be pissed on, built on the back of, scaled with brick, wood, to be lashed with rubber, tarred, to have your shale ribs cracked; to be sold, developed, shaped and reshaped by individuals, groups, soldiers, with witnesses, within earshot, under open windows, in your father's house; is to be exploded, chemicalled, dredged, mined, bombed, sheared, made a monument of; is to be tethered and tamed, mapped, photographed, marvelled at, shit on; is to be mowed, moved, monitored, circled, scoured; is to be made over, to be seen as passive, always, to bear the burden of resistance and maintenance, beginning and end, all in the folds of; to believe in special relationships: one breast all breasts; to mourn the drying up of milk, the tumorousness of nurture, the arms that surround nothing, the zero of once was, gone, past tense, now undeniably something else.

If only

If only men were more feminine. If only Judaism were more feminine. If only industry were more feminine. If only bridges were more feminine. If only trucks were more feminine. If only airplanes were more feminine. If only fruit were more feminine. If only engines were more feminine. If only economics were more feminine. If only test tubes were more feminine. If only physicists were more feminine. If only space were more feminine. If only Hollywood were more feminine. If only America were more feminine. If only farmyards were more feminine. If only the weather were more feminine. If only Islam were more feminine. If only engineers were more feminine. If only city planners were more feminine. If only feminists were more feminine. If only Catholicism were more feminine. If only politicians were more feminine. If only astronauts were more feminine. If only corporations were more feminine. If only women were more feminine. If only what was feminine were firm. If only there were slots. If only things fit inside.

If

If you open your mouth, ache. If you don't open your mouth, swelter. If you open your mouth but hold your breath, ether. If you look for colour, coral and tea leaves. If you follow the moon, wet and concrete. If you cling to the earth, pistol and candy apple. If you give up your garden, maze and globe, hydrangeas and moon vines. If you lose your shoes, pumice and strain. If you have no money, tin, linen, clang. If you lie down with dogs, pale and tender. If you watch television, carrot and yanking. If you embrace nothing, lustre and tar. If you know sorrow, whistle and salt. If you lie down with birds, currents and vertigo. If you breathe, corpuscular and crepuscule. If you can, software and lingerie. If you should, totem, forelock, tibia, stamen. If you are blonde, topple, flax, moraine. If you love flowers, do not fold. If you follow the sun, straw and oval. If you hide, velvet and myrrh. If you are a redhead, pepper and artichoke. If you eat only limes, Knossos and paddle. If you sing, ozone, crackle and stir. If you are wanting, scathed and shrouded. If you open your eyes, salt lick and clover. If you lie down with cats, ankle and dock. If you follow your heart, sledgehammer. If you embrace all, oarlock and tidal. If you look for light, spleen, splint. If you follow the earth, spade and compass. If you lie down with fish, ice cube and convection. If you know anger, detonate and flex. If you give up walls, columbine and feather. If you are still here, present and peel, dandelion and lemon hound.

ON THE SCENT

'It is too late to be simple.'

Lisa Robertson

1

Here she is inside. Walls and windows. Appendages and openings. Here she is sitting on a stack of books. Here she is digging out from under an avalanche of paper. Here she is swatting words with her coattails. Here she is wondering what to do with outdated memory. Here she is boxing and unboxing. Here she is moving stuff. Here she is deleting whole files, randomly. Here she is perplexed at the mounds of paper. Here, I tell you, here she is hiding under the Xerox machine. Here she is communing with resonators. Here she is clucking the MRI tune. Here she is earplugged and eyeshadowed. Here she is tall and long in the stride, here she is a force of circulation. Here she is sideways in a windstorm. Here she is teal and persimmon. Here she is Italian plum. Here she is the palest interior of the pomegranate. Here she is. Here she is in Banana Republic. Here she is black and black. Here she is thinking of the colour blue. Here she is trying to see underwater. Here she is reading on the train to New York. Here she is wiping coffee from the seat. Here she is sitting next to seven young rappers, pants like circus tents, durags and ball caps piled on high. Here she is. Here she is in an office in Philadelphia thinking of the letter R. Where would we be without R, she asks? Where would we be without E? Where would we be without arms? Here she is with meringue and milquetoast. Here she is hiding behind a maple tree in October, the weather having changed too quickly and she without a sweater. Here she is walking down Bleecker thinking, how? How? How can she describe the windmill of her aorta? How tibia is her confusion? How like the Microsoft song her frustration flits and crescendos. How like the blue of the xp screen her mood flickers in the traffic-jam hour. How archaic the need to open a window and breathe.

2

There she is outside the treatment centre on Nevins.
There she is geranium petals and struck matches.
There she is yelling into her cellphone. There she is
tangerine polyester, frills and net sleeves. There she is
gold-dusted cornrows. There she is in white heels,
beaks sharp on the pissed and gum-strewn sidewalk.
There she is, nails like beetles. There she is about to
kick some champagne-talking boy-ass. There she is,
gold-chained purse slung over sandstone shoulders.
There she is, her best friend's head punctuating with
uh huh and oo wee and *you go girl* and *ain't it so*. There
she is orchestrating particles of autumn, an unre-
strained refrain layered into the afternoon symphony
of boom-box rap and the mailman's soul tunes, the
dozen residents chain-smoking around the entrance,
the honk of suvs and delivery vans, the cussing out of
this one back using and that one found abusing.
There she is snapping words like stilettos into imagi-
nary crotch zones. There she is overtired, fed up,
caffeine wired, too many obligations expired. There
she is chewing up her anytime minutes for *this*? There
she is, ten seconds from despair, three feet from free-
dom, two dollars from a subway uptown where a new
job waits. There she is, one nod from a three-room flat
and a wardrobe from Lane Bryant, flying solo with her
kick-ass girls and a workout pass at the Y, her life crisp
as October, her life open and yappy, Fulton Street mall
on a Saturday after payday in the sunshine, bouncy as
a pocketful of twenty-dollar bills.

3

The girls run from one end of the paved playground to the other. In chadors they chase smaller boys who kick a soccer ball back and forth yelling *Can't play. Can't play.* The girls run and hurl themselves, landing again and again in each other's arms. The girls stop and yell *Let me kick!* The boys leap and leap into the air, legs cool in soccer shorts and Nikes. The girls in their long pants chase and are not distracted by hopscotch, not inclined toward chalk marks on pavement; they want the pleasure of skin in air, they want the satisfaction of forcing shapes against the sky. The boys kick against the fence where a small girl has cornered an even smaller girl and, one hand on her hip, the other poised to strike, scolds *How many times do I have to tell you, girl? How many times do I have to say? How many times do I have to slap you silly?* The smaller one slumped, face covered as the older one tongue-lashes and finally knees her in the face. The girls run past the yelling girl unfazed. The girls slam against the fence, fingers curled where moments ago sparrows perched to gulp crumbs from stale sandwiches. The girls stop and hang, undisturbed by the yelling. The girls look into each other's eyes. The girls fling their heads back and laugh.

4

The women plug themselves in. They work hard. They untwist bread bags and dole out dabs of butter. They choose low-fat milk. They have bought digital cameras. They join food co-ops. They find recycling sources. They mail things diligently. They see the sun as unlimited potential. Aureole and blister, thumbs and jelly, websites and manifestos. The women are red. They are preoccupied with shoes. They subscribe to green. Thoughts extend like awnings. Inscription and tongue, wireless cards and upgrades, the women circulate petitions. They forward articles about Björk and Rachel Corrie. They organize demonstrations, worry over hoarfrost on lemon groves. They delegate. They multi-task. The women press their foreheads against granite.

The women are blue. They consider heels an option. They have unplugged Ani and plugged in Radiohead. They are amused. They toast veggie dogs and buy organic; some of them embrace beef. They wear Birkenstocks, they smoke cigars, they wear their hair long or they shave it. They find time. They buy soy. They surf. They bookmark Bitch, Slut, Whore. They are sworn to transgress. They diss meatloaf and socks with sandals. They buy appliances. Everyone is witty. They blend fabrics. They make their own porn. They know the eighteenth century.

The women are burgundy. They discover obscure cases of women. They take notes. They take classes. They discover points of departure. They cut a wide swath. They dream of seducing Björk. They are not tongue-tied. They are not fooled by nature. They create gardens of air, orchid and oxalis. Some have discovered Lucinda Williams. They read Stein. They are not good girls. Some women are prismatic. Everyone is just liberal enough. The women often unplug themselves. They penetrate. They let their hair grow. They find a good masseuse. They have never read Mary Daly. They go shopping for shoes. They are divided by shoes. They cannot get over shoes. The shoes corral them. The groups divide further.

The women are pink. They shop for appliances. They fix cars and join car clubs. The women wave at each other across the gaps. They are always running out of batteries. The women strut and feather themselves. They buy hair products. They buy eye cream even if they love wrinkles. They have all read *The Handmaid's Tale* and tucked it away neatly. Despite everything, race continues to divide. The women are plugged in. The women carry their laptops into gardens. The women embrace only so much integration. Some women are salmon. Some women have turned in their diamonds for pens. The women have credit cards. They are relieved feminism is over. They are proud of their humour. They don't wear tampons lightly. They blend colours. They feel bad about

Martha Stewart. They have given up on Madonna. They meditate. They read. They don't do the right thing. They make gardens in matchboxes.

Miracles of green, they are mechanical. They find ways to breed with women. They start businesses, they discuss tax rates, pass on words of advice. They cajole and banter. They have potlucks. They are all disappointed with Hilary. They have barn raisings; no roof is too high, or too wide. Beam and lathe; hammer and throng. They masturbate and seduce. They have appliances and they know how to use them. They wear spaghetti straps and heels. They wear overalls and boots. They spit. They gesticulate. Their hair is shale and limestone. They attend lesbian baby showers. Civil and chardonnay: unbelievable cunning. They worry about footwear. They get excited about leather. They remember Barbie. They work out. They run. They do seven kinds of yoga. They buy magazines and try new diets. They consider law school. They are not afraid of engineering. They are great shoppers. They demand value.

The women are red. The women are full of themselves. The women kibbutz and spritz. They spin discs. They worry about piercing. They buy books online. They regret there is no more need for women-only spaces. They remember women's bookstores with only a tinge of regret. They are full bodied, they are sweltering, they are rock and graphite, purloined and vegan, heavy hipped and encyclopedic. They are annotated. They invite the optic. They embrace titanium. They shed their skin daily. Others gather it. There are bags of us in a basement. Earth is there too, aluminum, and feather.

5

The mothers were feminists. The mothers marched. The mothers wore purple and read Betty Friedan. The mothers listened to Janis Ian and Ferron. The mothers dropped out. The mothers went to Michigan and danced topless. The mothers used menstruation cups. The mothers tie-dyed everything and cooked meals from *Moosewood*. The mothers had committee meetings. The mothers subscribed to *Ms.* and believed in affirmative action. The mothers wore Birkenstocks and dreamed of living in Vermont or Saltspring. The mothers ate dried fruit and brown rice. The mothers lived in the suburbs and shopped. They fought to build credit ratings. The mothers wore sweater sets. The mothers knew nothing of feminism. The mothers ran off to Los Angeles. The mothers liked to sunbathe. The mothers discovered Paxil and Prozac. The mothers went to Holt's; they discussed Bloomingdale's and Saks. The mothers listened to Neil Diamond and sewed skirts. The mothers had sharp tongues. The mothers went to the opera. The mothers had good educations. The mothers had nothing to say. The mothers voted for Reagan or Mulroney. The mothers read *Newsweek* and *Cosmo*. The mothers read Alice Walker. The mothers held down two jobs, raised children and continued to believe. The mothers moved forward, hesitant, never sure what they had won, or what was merely yet to be revealed.

6

Years crimsoned before her. Windows appeared and were washed. White, the laundry clung to her magnetic feet. She meditated on the iron, willed permanent press into existence. Sunday mornings the hallways hollow. Prayer books like paperweights. Cotton wool and cotton wool. Maternity ward as spa weekend. Moods flat as pancakes. Afternoons brief as half a Valium. Fish-tank calm. Years appearing like stains on the sheets. There was once a convertible and winding mountain roads. There was once a sapling waistline. There was talk of California. Padded and padded her life of Kotex corsets. Ankles exposed and pellet breasts. Years soft as spaniel ears. Swells and churning. The big book of prescription drugs. The doctors' bible. Bookends of days. *True Romance. True Confessions. True Stories.* Muffled and muffled. Curious: *Alfred Hitchcock Presents.* Her life between two fingers. Her life cracking on porcelain. Years arbouring opaque, crystalline. Asbestos and asbestos. Aperture closing. Underexposed, unmerited. Hours slippery as newborns. Days hard as nails. Years heavy as rain clouds. Her head an oven. Puppet mouth and marionette of limbs. Skin thin as foil. Drawbridge flimsy. Moat of heels. Lockless, braless, the patina of possibility. Gods shimmering in the altar of kitchen. The echo of her mind filled with pipe cleaners and devil's food. Years with the crusts cut off. Pink and bite sized. The footstool of her back, blue vinyl: easy to clean.

7

Yes there is mink. Some women in silk. Yes there are seamstresses. Some women never see daylight. That woman in the Campbell's soup factory. That woman with her gold watch and osteoporosis. She was the wife of a professor. She gave dinner parties. That one arrived Tuesdays and cleaned the bathroom. This one knows how to polish silver and recite Akhmatova. That one has a man stubborn as ink. Yes there is linen. Some women in wool. That one is being called to the bar. Oh there are burkas. That one is cowed by her seven-year-old son. That one is beaten by her son-in-law. That one has twenty-two siblings back in Cuba. Yes there is cashmere. Some women shop on Fifth Avenue. That woman stapling leather armchairs. That woman collecting cigarette butts. Oh for a diamond pendant and worsted wool. Victoria's Secret and Seventh Avenue. There is nothing to tell about. That one counting pills. That one ringing in. That one limping through Penn Station with a broken heel. Oh there are days she could forget. This one falls asleep on the subway. This one is considering infanticide. This one will do anything to avoid her mother. She is meeting her husband's best friend's wife at a hotel in Midtown. She is selling batteries, a dollar for two. These three belt Motown on the subways every afternoon between one and three. Oh for Italian cookware. Oh for those new Manolo Blahniks. That one has a tongue like a lobster. She hasn't seen her family in forty years.

8

Yes there are coupons to clip. Yes I've been to Filene's. Yes I have stood in the shadow of the Eiffel Tower. Yes I've tried tempeh. Yes on a camel, on a horse and once while looking at an iguana. Yes I collect Air Miles. Yes I voted for Clinton. Yes with my cat, always after a busy day. Yes I've been to the Brooklyn Macy's. Yes in the CN Tower. Yes while listening to Tom Waits. Yes, yes, yes in the desert with a man in tasselled shoes. Yes I said tassels. Yes in the Tower of London. Yes I sometimes cook and do the dishes. Yes in the changing room at Lord & Taylor. Yes with a cousin in a photo booth in Vancouver. Yes on a 747. Yes in my grandmother's house. Yes in a car parked on the mountain. Yes in Snohomish. Yes in Summerland. Yes, yes, yes with Anais Nïn. Yes I've tried the Atkin's. Yes I've lost fifteen pounds. Yes I feel great about it. Yes I can feel my ribs. Yes when I bend over I imagine Johnny Depp's hands on my hips. Yes I have eaten raw meat. Yes I have hiked in the Laurentians. Yes, yes, yes I can find my way home. Yes with a zucchini. Yes with a water gun shaped like an eggplant. Yes there are good deals to be had. Yes I've thrown up. Yes I've considered suicide. Yes Todd Solondz gives me nightmares. Yes I've overdrawn my account. Yes, yes, yes I have a crush on Stockard Channing. Yes in a turret. Yes in a Chevy. Yes on the beach in La Jolla. Yes while reading Chekhov. Yes in a parking lot in Denny's. Yes on the turnpike. Yes in satin. Yes I think Cate Blanchett is hot. Yes in 501s. Yes women in wedding dresses turn me on. Yes with a bride. Yes with a groom. Yes with a brother and sister. Yes while watching porn. Yes with peaches. Yes in the blackout serenaded by sopranos. Yes insufferable in surf. Yes in the pantry while the poker game peaked. Yes in stilettos. Yes in flats. Yes in pink plastic. Yes you do. Yes I will. Yes while there's still time. Yes while I can. Yes whenever possible. Yes I'll be a top. Yes I'll be your bottom. Yes I'll whomp your ass. Yes after shopping. Yes with chocolate. Yes now. Yes here. Yes even alone.

9

Oh, she said, the ladies of Boston never tipped their hats. Nor did hemlines flirt with pubic hair. There was never enough ice. She would never have an above-ground pool. We never spoke at dinner. We never talked of money. We never said *sex*. There were never any fluids. The women were buttoned down. The women took Ex-Lax and subscribed to *Good Housekeeping*. And the white women in Tuscaloosa never sit next to blacks. Oh, she said, you're from Canada? I'm so sorry.

10

This is a perfectly good girl. If ever there wasn't. They curried and peaked under. Mountains of foam. Everyone wondered at once. Tiny, they imagined, saran wrapped in denim. Pink Floyd and green tequila Jell-O. Condomed Barbie dolls dunked in SpaghettiOs. They brushed by and were furious. Insertion. Penetration. Tipsy, they peered in and retreated. They gathered in rec rooms with men resembling Peter Frampton and David Bowie. Sherry with her Lees bent at the knees. After school Sheila and Lane serving Pink Ladies while they videoed. How he handled himself. How he liked to show them *Playgirl*s. Penises cinnamon and arced on thighs. How suburban. How late–twentieth century. How the girls bumped up against each other giggling. How they tittered. How they scurried. Feathered hair wisping around freckled cheeks. Dawn collected bus transfers. Sherry took up soccer. Donna beneath the sheets. Oh girls in the school-yard swinging. Dogwood and Disney matinees. Friday night dry discos. Dry humping. Shivering on the underleaf of teen. Cigarettes folded in cotton underwear. Vodka in Coke cans. Everyone wanting the black boys to dance. This is a perfectly good girl. This is a perfectly fine night. This is a perfectly ordinary suburb. Michelle with her flat tummy always trying to go down. Girls to be pried. French kissing. Jeans tight and bumping. Mall girls hanging around potted plants under skylights. Mall girls drinking

Orange Julius and snarking at housewives. Girls with slingshot wit. Girls with knife-blade morality. Girls in cords window-shopping. Girls being driven home from babysitting a hand sliding up the thigh. Girls curious and tangled as kittens. Girls with training bras and lipstick. Girls sitting on volcanoes. Girls who bite off more than they can eschew.

11

This happened before. Then we ran. And the cable hooked us to a big dish. We signed up for more. Golden arches nosed up out of concrete and we were delighted. Everyone bought a Ford or Chrysler. Roads appeared and women disappeared down them. Millions were served. Some of them waved. This happened before. Then again maybe not. Anyhow once we walked to the television. Once your little sister stood and changed the channel from two to three, one hand on the antenna. This really happened. Sometimes topless. At the end of the line there was a person. Whole lives ticked by on salaries. Everyone wore polyester blouses with imprints of European landmarks. People dialed and the numbers rumbled like a bank vault. Shag appeared in avocado green and harvest gold penetrating every corner. Coffee tables thickened overnight. Lights morphed into plastic balls hung from chains. Little girls rhymed couplets, index finger poised, waiting for the plastic rotary to hit zero. This really happened. Women clicking on manual typewriters. Whole offices of *scritch, scritch, scritch* and *ping, ping, ping* as the carriage released and rolled up. How we embraced the correctable ribbon. How we coveted whiteout. Listen, once people sent letters with words crossed out. This all happened. People placed vinyl on turntables and lifted needles, jumping slightly when the scratch blared out of the cross-hatched speakers from RadioShack or Sears. Rumours of a

Japanese takeover surfaced. There was talk of importing fathers. Then again maybe I am lying. Anyone knew it was true. Anyhow we didn't run. We bought bigger cars and women embraced the muumuu. Everything was arriving all at once. Lapels like pizza slices. Soul music sweetened the air. People drove their cars to drive-ins and hung metal speakers on the side windows. Oh, how we embraced the wire.

12

Oh and it was a matter of time before someone yanked it tight. Oh and it was a matter of time before someone started chopping things in half. Oh and turn public into private. Oh and doors slammed. Oh and suddenly stocks. Oh and suddenly he got that idea. Oh and everything outside becomes inside. Oh and economies of scale. Oh and put what's inside outside. Oh and components. Oh and change. Oh and break down and break down and break down and oh who wouldn't rather have? Oh and ever smaller pieces. Oh and can't you see where I'm heading with this? Oh and Middle East and Vietnam like wicks. Oh and what was outside comes in. Oh first public becomes private, then private becomes public. Oh and embrace change for its own sake, change. Oh and soon enough every man a nation, every household GNP and GDP and export and import. Oh and don't forget the wire. Oh and the way he struck the match. Oh and the how of it combusting. It's like this: Once there was a channel and a city. Once there were jobs that fed a town and once there was agriculture. Once there was mixed-use land and people came and went with quarts of raspberries and blueberries. Schools were built without metal detectors. Once the local news was local. Once *Playboy*s were hidden under daisy-print comforters. Once there were neighbours. Oh and once people walked. Oh and once they had picnics in the park and once they went to the local swimming pool and once they knew where their food was grown and once things came whole and once you knew where your child's teacher was from and once, and once, and once.

13

Listen there was a time. Listen we all knew. Listen it was so fast. Listen there was a wall and the wall would not fall. Listen we ate Twizzlers and watched Clint Eastwood and Burt Reynolds. Listen a whole generation believed Herbie the Love Bug flew. Listen no one knew any better. Listen no one saw it coming. The wire, the wire, the why are, the why are. The why are we here? Listen there was time. There was a beginning. There was a moment of reflection. There was elongation and fattening. There was a place to gather. There was something before this. There was that other. There were hallways and cooking smells. There were people who wrapped furniture. There were whole rooms unused. There was a belief in place. There was a notion of time. There was a way. That was before. Now things are otherwise.

14

The tummy-flat girls will not embrace feminism. Will not consider ecology or philosophy anything more than a brand name. They are not worried about the environment, a luxury for another generation. A pre–bubble bursting time. They are so done with all that. They are so over it. They are so *Whatever*. They are so *Yeah, yeah, yeah*. They are so *She's so uptight*. They are so *She's such a nightmare*. They are so *Bummer*. They are so bored. They have so little time for that. They are so done with earnest. They are so *PC is a university credit*. They are so *I wanna sit on his face*. They are so *I want to give head where I want when I want*. They are so *Isn't sexism sexy?* They are so *Boys are just built like that*. They are so *Being gay is passé*. They are so *How could you be so mean?* They are so *What planet are you from?* They are so done with the whiny girls. They are so done with political messages. They are so past any need to protest. They are so *What's your problem?* They are so *We're fine with the way things are*. They are so *That's just the way it is*. They are so *Get over it*. They are so *Accept it*. They are so *Anger is so uncool*. They are so *Move out of our way rigid one, and let the beautiful ones sing*.

VIRGINIA, VANESSA, THE STRANDS

'Many bright colours; many distinct sounds; some human beings, caricatures; comic; several violent moments of being, always including a circle of the scene which they cut out: and all surrounded by a vast space – that is a rough visual description of childhood.'

Virginia Woolf

'The further one goes toward the past, the more indissoluble the psychological memory-imagination mixture appears.'

Gaston Bachelard

Everything approaching and then disappearing, getting large, getting small, passing at different rates of speed

They are in the nursery waiting to be saved. There is a window pull banging against a wall. A small acorn. The smell of bread queases her. The day is long. There is sand in the sheets. Someone is digging in the asparagus bed (they still are). There are hands and there are hands. Once they praised women. Where is he now? Everyone needs to wait. They must suffer appropriately, but they must not make one feel bad. There must be just enough. Once women carried water. The curtains rise and fall. We must all be patient. Soon there will be letters. Soon there will be food. Once women roamed. Once women wore animal skins. Now there must be walls. There must be houses, tall and thin, with corners to hold memories and windows to frame things. There must be containment.

I should make curved shapes, showing the
light through, but not giving a clear outline

Many shapes. Sudden ruptures of joy. Exalted lashes
of light stroking the wall, there up toward the
cornice, down to unknown voices in the garden. All
this a state of rapture despite the cool feel of marble
on bare skin. Lines being drawn. There on the ceil-
ing one's future scissors. Below voices. Nowhere
safer. Moments rife as opium. Moments to break
open. Moments later to stroke and stoke. Moments
of balm, moments delicious and staggering, hooks of
story, daggers and parachutes, exit wounds, door-
ways, boulders weighing and releasing; boulders to
stand on and trip over, moments, make of them what
you will.

The buzz, the croon, the smell, all seemed to press voluptuously against some membrane

In the garden there are streamers. The streamers catch light. Iridescent, chiffonesque, they twist, ruby and emerald lures. The girls linger. They are caught by the murmur of bees. Geranium and honeysuckle. Not yet bloomed, the poppies are vulgar. Vanessa reaches out to touch one. Paint might improve them. Virginia is appalled. Virginia stands back. She can't take her eyes off them. There is something lacking. There is something she has not heard. There is something sticking about the ears. She circles around. Has she seen a poppy before? She wants to reach out. Wants to press her nose, ears, back of her hand but she can't bring herself to touch them. The poppies are not angry. They nod like pepper. They wink at the sun. They lean into each other. They are downcast. They are swollen eyed. There are pearls of water on them. They are raw and wanting. They peer out from shrouds of thorn. They pry the air. The sun is afraid of them; suddenly she is sure of this, panicked in the garden, frozen. Vanessa has come around. Vanessa says poppies are the eyes of children. She says they contain real life. Virginia will not have it, but now she is lubricated once more, now she can move. Virginia sees the ants on the poppies. The ant is sucking at the droplet of water on the unbloomed poppy, turning and turning the whole garden in his eye. She looks closer and a slit of red appears. The red is violent. It presses against the seam like a tongue. The red is dizzying. The red tenses her body. The red is folded and bursting. The red is paper-thin. She feels it in her head, in her hands, in other folds. She will fade into the sun. If she does not move she will not exist. The red is like a parachute. The red will unfold like a paper lantern. Like the poppy, she has not yet unfurled. The poppies will float across the garden, taking her out of childhood. She is dizzy with waves of heat. They lap like a hot sea in the yard. She squints and is underwater. The poppies are sea anemones. The peonies are jellyfish. A fin appears in the distance and she must steady herself. *Where is your hat?* She has no hat and the sun is hot. She opens her eyes. The poppies are still closed. She will stand until they are open. She has never seen a poppy open. Another ant appears on the nut-like head. There are smaller ants too. Climbing the forest of fuzz. They circle the small head. Virginia can't tear herself from the poppy. Vanessa is amused. Vanessa is impatient. Vanessa wants the poppies to unfold, she thumbs the slit and Virginia is appalled. Virginia understands something about holding back. Her presence does nothing to encourage. There is no understanding between them. If she stands another moment the air will explode her lungs, but she is not under water. She is not in the sea. *That is whole*, she says. *That is whole.*

There was the moment of the puddle in the path

And the puddle was the word. And the puddle reflected everything. And the puddle grew. And the puddle spoke back. And the puddle was nothing. The puddle unplugged her. It drained her. And the puddle was silent. The puddle went on forever, it struck fear in her. And the puddle was thin and spreading. The puddle spoke Greek and the puddle knew all. The puddle wore britches. It knew precisely what she was thinking. And the puddle sunk deeper. And the puddle haunted. And the puddle grew before her. And the puddle divined the word. And the puddle engulfed her. And the puddle made her still. And the puddle made her grow tall. And the puddle froze her. The puddle scorned. It laughed. The puddle meant business. The puddle threatened. The puddle reached out. The puddle snatched at her ankles. The puddle was monstrous. The puddle had hands. The puddle was mundane. The puddle smelled of spring. The puddle contained five volumes of the lives of the poets; it carried paper sailboats. The puddle was a birdbath. The puddle was filled with tadpoles. The puddle went on forever. The puddle was bottomless; it contained the cosmos. The puddle smelled like cocoa. Beetles swam in it. Cotton wool gathered. Ants bathed. The puddle was dirty. The puddle reflected everything. The puddle embraced her. The puddle saw up her skirt. The puddle shamed her. The puddle was a mirror. The puddle shattered her. The puddle was larger than life. The puddle was irreverent. The puddle needed to be put in its place.

A man sitting on the edge of the bed

Hesitation upon seeing. A little lack in the middle.
A long way out. Something to reach, something to
ward us off. A long time coming. Reaching only.
Seeing the end there. Nothing less than never again.
Lips on iron. Impression of succession, Stella lean-
ing down to undo a button on her nightgown, lips
upright, iron and nowhere to be seen. No further.
Turret walls and moat of nursery. The solid core.
Upended. Emptied. Wrapped in towels. Led with
brandy. Led into the great room. Led down the hall.
Led to the bed, lips on iron. Led, led, led, always ever
after the expectation, the kiss in the garden, the kiss
of iron. Led where he is standing. Led where he
would have us go. Always after. Led. Led. Led.

The sleeping side was dominated by the long
Chippendale (imitation) looking glass, given
me by George in the hope that I should look
into it and learn to do my hair and take
general care for my appearance

There in a long line. There *those long solitary mornings
reading Greek*. A thousand years. Many bright virgins
handed down. The brides of left-wanting. Bread
pudding. Not always in the parlour. Not always in the
nursery. Found out by the soft wax. Always a man
hovering. Sprinkle of words in the sheets. Even on
the deathbed, fingers reaching out. A long line.
There in a long line. Illicit reading by the light of a
candle. Illicit thinking by the hand going under. The
brides of left-wanting. Rooks gliding over this house
going under. There in a long line. There he found
her. There with cats crying in the alley and a beggar
breaking into the garden. Under the gaze of George
with his stash of spent light bulbs like bombs flying
over the garden wall, there now a rooming house,
now planes passing over, now bombs hurled over
bigger walls, while there snuggled, there snuggled,
there in a long line.

And in the days I speak of, god, faun and pig
were … alive, all in opposition, and in their
conflicts producing the most astonishing
eruptions

White scuffing folding in white hands the light scissoring after yet another ball. Fragrant of slit-eyed something mewing. Nothing jagged in white and the dark interior of Virginia Creepers. What did you say Nessa? Where does the stamen fit? Walls of Watts and busts hushing unnatural gloom of a room. Here insulated, here spice buns and tea. Circle of a scene cut. Light gone out. Scuttling, scuttling. Make nothing of it. Making much of him golden as Hermes in a Kensington drawing room. And aren't women always in dim spaces with the lights off? Aren't women always holding out? Oh how they ripen like plums dangling overhead luscious and firm. After all there are diamonds and silk stockings. Everything is pleasant. Who needs to be copying out Greek letters? Who needs to know? The world is detail. The world is lighted candles and opera boxes. White scuffling how he advanced with his opera hat. Must break out of this sentence. Must lift off the asphyxia of words, words, each of them laden, each of them musty and clinging; each one a medal, gleaming on his chest. How they lull me. How there is a sense of going under. How they lay upon me like flattened wool. Muffle man, muffling. The cook serving up pig's feet. How he kneeled in front of women, adoring, imploring, how his layering goes on.

MEANWHILE, ELSEWHERE, OTHERWISE

'Everything makes spaces.'

Gertrude Stein

Moments ripe as cherries

She puts one foot in front of the other. One word in front of the other as she motors down State Street past the Orthodox church where tradesmen, backs buckling, plane a gothic door, thinking *I am no longer young. I am no longer thin. Words have gained weight. They gather at the waist. Tangle around the ankles. How to untangle and venerate? How to tell? One word is all it takes, others being willed to follow.* And she is off, arms and alms along for the ride, mind galloping before her, sniffing at the hem of one boy in an oversized Curtis Brown T-shirt iPod wired.

One word, one foot, her great coat swerving this way and that, the shadow and swing of the past, the glittering present, the Merlin of perception. This is what she means: moments sliding like oysters on the tongue, salty and filled with the dreams of whales. Moments spread thick as peanut butter. Moments silky and curved as the Queen Anne armchair she sat in Sunday on Lafayette. Could it fit in the sitting room? Could she carry that too?

There is a hum in her ear when the wind passes; her thoughts wing the air, nestle in window boxes, peer down at her in Sly leather, glory of geranium, light so nutmeg and soupy the tip of her tongue responds.

Threading and threading she is thinking that this moment corresponds to pan-fried zucchini blossoms. For no reason they collide in the air and she comes to a stop outside the chain-linked bamboo garden. Here even gardens are padlocked, double padlocked, razor-wired, triple chained: New Yorkers heavy with keys rattling through the subway. She thinks of the garter snakes napping under potato leaves, the deer nibbling on bush beans, rain collecting in the crevices of leaves (long ago, long ago), her tentative walking to the garden, her sense of impermanence.

Have you come in? Have you come?
(Yes I have but I am not in which is a pity.)
There she thinks
                    the end of commas. The end

§

Still there are people who walk on earth. Her foot taps the concrete, pulls at the chain link wondering who has the key?

To whom might she inquire about walking on earth?

§

She is here she is now she is no more than the memories clanging like tin cans behind her. On and on she pushes past the rent-a-buggy, and Smith Street to State and Boerum where there is a widening. A suburban flattening. Cars hungry for the Brooklyn

Bridge which she considers crossing now considers (reconsiders) the long trek north cold and clear and beckoning. But no. Sad suddenly. Perhaps there is no there

there.

§

Meanwhile we must wait. We must wait for time to unfold. We must stand in front of Chase Manhattan and consider umbrellas. We must be sensible in tainted leather. We must insist on the moment nothing more than the present moment. How perfect to bend down and pick up the Doritos bag the Odwalla bottle dropped at one's feet because we can because it is our concrete as much as anyone's. She mutters *Love the concrete. Love the car that cuts across. Love the man who brushes your ass, toothless and smelling of subways.* Noise is a symptom of poverty but not in Manhattan. She says this to no one in particular and no one in particular responds.

§

Because there is a there

there

we

find ourselves now anywhere but here which is nowhere near where we think we are. Otherwise now. There is certainly a place. A place that calls out.

A place that slips in between noun and verb. Several moments begin to bleed. Panicked she mistook the sky. She mistook the weather. Her intentions were good. Whether or weather there were some interruptions on the horizon that wanted her attention. She took up her palette. She hit *Send*.

§

When crossing borders it is best to be firm. The otherwise of fluidity. There are several varieties of mushrooms one had best not eat. This is not true of vowels. Information so rarely corresponds. Is so rarely of use. She considers. (She was always looking back. She never did.) Consonants certainly demand one's attention. (Consonants require cabs.) *When a word has two Ts they both need acknowledgement* says the man from the Paris Opera. (There she was sitting in the seventeenth row nodding.) *Otherwise stutter.* Suddenly she stumbles stares cement curb. Familiar and yet on and on it goes. Here

on and on the line will go and she after it. (Behind her landscapes unravelling.) She wants to upend herself now unravel on the boardwalk spin into lower Manhattan. Certainly one could begin again. This is a poem underway! Any moment! Neon. Any moment sense!

§

Still it comes out. Even if it comes out ugly it is still out. She had several things to say sitting where she was on the cold bench. Now snow. Now freezing. Now thaw. Now the East River with its dead cats and billion unheard words a bottomless thud. Say.

Say what?

               that. There it comes. That thing you recognize. There it comes now. There it comes. Now. Bring the glass to your lips. There.

Some other poet in the city

In another poem a woman might let memories solid-
ify, and as they hardened beneath her, step on them
one and one and one until she left the old world
neatly behind. In another poem death. In another
poem light. In another poem there is no E in heart.
In another poem there is an H. In another poem feel-
ing is orchestrated. In another poem a woman might
find pleasure in the sound of her own words, might
feel quite naturally content with herself, see the city
as a pleasant backdrop. In another poem a woman
might couplet. In another poem a woman might
villanelle. In another poem squeaky clean. In
another poem tidy. In another poem, pause, and
pause. In another poem sestina. In another poem
concrete. In another poem sound. In another poem
squander. In another poem a woman might do a
handstand on a patch of grass the only grass for
miles but her mind rests the whole of Wyoming
under her thumb.

Some other poets and the puddle

'When for no reason I could discover, every-
thing suddenly became unreal.'

Virginia Woolf

She didn't notice the puddle. She was busy unravel-
ling the pavement. She clip-clopped past. She had
serious business. The words in her head were pleas-
ing her. She liked the sun. The smell of meat sizzling
called out. Language needed to be parted, ordered.
The children irritated her as they played in the
puddle. They were noisy. It was not her business.
There were no books in the playground, but there
were shapes to things. Sentences combusted. No
one recognizes. The words in her head grew cold.
They needed a rest. Her feet had an idea. She
thought they meant business. She saw herself in
everything and everything was good.

She saw the puddle as pewter. She swallowed it sweet
as figs. She saw it nestled in the cleavage of plum
girls. She held them over her head and cracked their
legs.

She saw the universe in the puddle. She saw a slide
show of organic compounds. She saw the key and the
key fit. She saw the genital-less amoeba as a hero.
She put her ear to the puddle but she was no naïve
child; she was listening for the rumble of trucks, not
the sweet musings of water beetles.

She waited until winter and when the puddle froze over, she glided across it. She sat in the summer heat and was content. She lifted the puddle and slid it down her arm like a pancake. She invited a girl gang over and drank it. She had no puddles on her street. She had no street. She leapt over the puddle on horseback in pursuit. She saw streams of Nazis skimming boot black across the surface. She thought she heard the apostles and so kneeled down to pee. She dove in, scraping her nose. She had her father drain all the puddles in the village. She splashed. She leapt and bombed it with rocks. She floated the toppled heads of Barbie dolls. She walked around. Then she walked around again. She heard men flinging mud and arranged a blanket of oak leaves across the surface. She did a cartwheel. She knit a scarf out of the letters R and E which she wound round and round and round.

Or: another way of telling

'The quality of the air above Talland House
seemed to suspend sound.'

Virginia Woolf

1

The squeak of the hinge the rooks this moment the
sounds all of them winding round the house wheel-
barrow lawnmower poplar leaves cawing brooms
knocking dresses rustling a plank alone

every footstep quick voice cheerful then
low (she must be talking to a child) when

suddenly gruff murmur

irregularly broken by the taking out of pipes and the
putting in of pipes which had kept on assuring her
monotonous fall of

which for the most part beat a measured
and soothing consolingly oh monotonous
over and over again
ephemeral then suddenly a loud cry
as of a sleepwalker
half roused apprehensively to see if anyone heard
him – ridiculous he a failure?

dully ominously entire joy

the pure joy of the two notes murmuring stamping and crowing until she

      to say good night and found them netted in their cots like birds among cherries and raspberries still making up stories about some little bit of solitude laying hold of some little odd or end. She listened

      still

        cricket children baths sea melancholy had never Lily was listening Mrs. Ramsay was listening they were all listening. Lamentation suffusion hailing him his voice his emphasis his uneasiness the movement of a trout when

      at the same time one can see the ripple and the gravel something to the right something to the left the whole now she said nothing. Words floating like flowers on the perfectly indifferent chill night air murmured *Steer, hither steer your winged pines, all beaten Mariners* her husband slapping his thighs.

2

Rubbing the glass leering sideways at her swinging figure a sound issued from her lips woman robbed of meaning the voice of witlessness persistency as she lurched dusting wiping gossiping ominous sounds hammers dulled cracked tea cups glass tinkled agony tumblers [a shell exploded] chaos streaked tumbling leviathans whose brows are melodies irregular never fully harmonized still room would break

      Lily Briscoe stirring in her sleep.

3

This first morning with the Ramsays

blankness of mind until these vapours had shrunk. *Alone, Perished* words wrote themselves all over the grey-green (as the waves) the immense pressure of his concentrated woe: she couldn't paint couldn't create words – no longer aware who originally spoke them. Ten ships driven into the bay for shelter mournful words

leaf upon leaf incessantly upon his brain voices harsh hollow sweet brooms tapping the wash and hush of the sea roar and crackle boastful she was surprised to find the old man had not heard her cry the eddy slackened the world full of little creaking squeaking as if they were anchored. Had he heard? Death mumbled

knitting stopped sounded hoarse on the stones

falling

drops a kind of hushing and hissing as if they were wild were perfectly free

tossed tumbled surged blurred answered without saying and

fluttering slowly

at length upon the earth.

STILL AND OTHERWISE

Later

The phones stopped ringing. Later there were biscuits and tea. The light settled on her brow and she opened the marmalade. There were letters from overseas. She remembered her grandfather, the schmearer. It was a temporary occupation. She didn't want her partner's hand on her thigh then. Just at the point of remembering, it is personal. *He schmeared leather*, she said. Her partner imagined him in a marketplace in London. *No*, she said, *Manchester. He smoked as he worked. He was always smoking.* They nibbled and poured, nibbled and poured. Sounds romantic. *It wasn't.* The light shifted and the little rattlebox of her heart sank. There was never any meaning. Morning fell like raindrops. Her partner fussed about the hair on her legs. She enjoyed smoothing the sheets. Later they went running. They did sit-ups and crunches. Shape was possible. Her partner was hopeful. A thin, angry man had cut her hair too short, still she believed. They had eggs florentine and laughed about summer. She told jokes sharp as an egg cracking. The punch lines sunk into the bowl, waiting to be whisked. Days drifted from the east. There were moments they doubted. What was his name, she wanted to know. *Who?* The schmearer. *Ah, it was Martin.*

The boys of Smith Street

Stop at Caruso's for a slice. They plumb the Falls for sources to hang paintings. They meet lovers at LULUc. The boys of Smith Street have carefully mussed hair. They drive Vespas and on hot nights drink beer at Bar Tabac. The boys of Smith Street wear jeans and white T-shirts. They hang out at Ziad's and smoke cigars. The boys of Smith Street push strollers and buy discs from Halcyon; they discuss screenplays and lyrics. The boys of Smith Street wear their pants too loose; buckles hang around their thighs and mothers are tempted to haul them up, give a cuff on the back of the head. The boys of Smith Street smack hands and drop b-balls at the corner. The boys of Smith Street cannot resist snow-balling pedestrians. The boys of Smith Street hoot, they are *Hey, hey,* and *Whassup?* They wear hoodies and smoke. They charge twenty dollars to dig out your car. They skateboard, dreads tucked under wool caps. The boys of Smith Street weave in and out of traffic on scooters. They lean and loaf at dusk watching cars pass. They adjust their Mets and Knicks caps. They read the *Voice* on Bergen. They run for the F train. They are perfumed and coiffed, they have soft nails, they wear their hair long. They are always moving, even when they stand still.

Meditation on a swallow and one peony

June was a river rock. They worried about ticks. Everyone had forgotten Iraq. The women from Niger were cold. Someone said there would be chocolate. The night before they heard poems based on the *I Ching*. People dreamed in Chinese characters and were baffled. She dreamed of a wall that wound and flexed its way through people's chests. It was only visible for two seconds each morning but she could not remember which two seconds. In the garden the poppies were shameless. Dazed honeybees emerged purple. She thought that if there were a wall she might see it here. The swallow looked sympathetic but she was only waiting. She made a gurgling sound just before her mate arrived. The swallow was sharp. She kicked off like a swimmer. They passed each other like balloons popping. It was not aware of any walls, but she was. She took a photo of dew on lupines. The peony was such a rich burgundy she could smell wine. The blue of the swallow hurtled overhead. They were arrows that ribboned the sky and made her miss home.

Sumac leaves laid around a hole

Burning. Rocks, leaves, calling out to him. Nothing existing on its own. His hand there, drawing attention to itself. Acts of enclosure. Who is taking a position? The world as pantry. The world as spice cupboard. The world labelled and labelled. This is not image. Is a line drawn on its own? What transforms a ring of sumac leaves? What moment? There are openings and openings. Nothing arbitrary. Buddhist ring, the sumac burns Tibetan: gold through crimson. The sumac is royal in its offerings. Wanting order there. No stories. A hole. Gopher, snake? Who is a portal? Telling about. A fissure burning to be ringed. Leaves longing to overlap. Does he hear them murmuring for his caress? There and there his hand, shaping, snapping.

The wall

All he knows is the wall winds through us. Wagon tracks exist a hundred years after the journey. Footsteps carbon dated. Who formed who? Things are wedged. Is this finding or being found? There are objects embedded. Unearthed. He is not a man who thinks rocks tell stories. Where the wall was. There was never any need. This rock bruises the earth. This wall dodges. It wends. This wall divorces whole families of trees. It confuses squirrels. Deer leap over it. Snakes fit themselves into its crevices. There was a time. There are gaps. For a hundred miles. Everything partitioned. Trees found in limestone. Prayer as vista. Stations of the stone. The wall encloses nothing. The wall encloses everything. The wall divides and the wall brings together. The wall rustles fall leaves. It blends. Fortify who? Give who a foundation? The men lay stones and it is good. Now the crows are content. There was never any doubt in the hummingbird's mind. Seen from the air everything has purpose. Knowing nothing keeps us centred. What we think about lays tracks in the mind. There are thoughts not yet discovered. They lie dormant as boulders. We move around them, shyly. Someone, please, show us the way in.

Headache, a pastoral

The Green Mountains hump toward Quebec. She takes off her hat and lies on the bed. Someone has screwed her jaw closed. There are forceps on her skull. Static pools in the hollows of her eyes. She is sure the Iceman died of a headache. They found fungi in his stomach. They say he had a toothache, still she suspects. She dare not walk by the river today. Not with her head pounding. Headaches kill, she thinks. Even now she imagines her head lying against the smooth river rock, the chill and massage of currents. She tries Advil and Stein. The room does not spin but she feels the car bumping all the way to Nancy. The light remains dull. The book ends. There is no rest. There are those who have headaches, she thinks. She walks into town for breakfast at the Plum Café, depressed to have left Gertrude and Alice who never complain of headaches. A toothless fisherman sits, a Rockwell at the counter. Men discuss ATVs. Her headache has followed her across the little bridge and into town. It sits with her at the counter. It follows her back across the little bridge barking behind her up the stairs. Maybe headaches are an English thing. She tries Tylenol and Woolf. There's some commiseration. She sits in the big armchair in her office thinking about rooks and gardens. Leonard off to Lytton's for a month with headache. Lush trees manicured. There are headaches, she thinks. And then there is headache.

Our Lady of Bark

Our Lady of Bark weaves the hunter into the wood. Sees birch as a breastplate. Forest of Amazons. She sleeps on boulders. Nothing whispers to her. She is not simply labelling. Not rearranging, not nature as Ikea, fitting. She is unlocking. Not special knowledge, but entering into. Revealing. Given time she would weave trees into skin. Given time trees would sprout feet and enter Manhattan. All the granite from Vermont would call out for a reunion. There are stranger things. We pass by daily. There is a place for bark, she says, and it is tender.

On the way to the swimming hole

She passes the watch-repair shop with its grandfather clock door. No one goes in or out but a dog barks. She is sure the repairman has never heard of Dali. Buttercups wave and bob. They are so yellow they shine a halo six inches around each pinky-sized flower. They are so good she wants to eat them, but they are singing, all along the roadside, and she cannot eat anything that sings.

A lilac begins to leaf

Last night the memory of her mother walked out into the parking lot of the Long Rail Tavern at precisely five minutes to twelve. Where her tears fell, tiny puffs of dust. X-ray her now you will see her mother filing her nails. Her heart flickers off and on, random as a cat's paw. She will not fall to pieces here. Though at least if she did, she could now put herself together again. She remembers a superhero made of boulders. He could assemble and reassemble. She could get bigger, she thinks. There might be room for two. And in her mind a lilac begins to leaf.

Ms. Forrest, ten years after

When I see you it is winter. You are pulling out of a parking spot in your old English roadster – blue, in my dream at least, a Blue Betty you say. I have never seen you in winter. I know there is nothing winter about you or where you live. Yet when I see you it is through the windscreen, wipers pushing at the heavy, wet snow. I come around the side of Betty, laughing. *There you are again*, I say. *A good winter?* you ask. *Not too cold.* What is it about you and winter, Ms. Forrest? On Saltspring, where if it snows I am sure it is only in prop-sized proportions. Why are you always pulling out of that spot? Leaning your head out to smile at me. Never stopping to spend time.

The smugglers

Two by two the smugglers line up along the shore, well-wrapped stashes of Levis and Adidas balanced on their heads. From the tiny Spanish enclave of Ceuta on the African coast, they enter the Mediterranean. Fully clothed, they stretch into the water like a swim class, each with their paddleboard of illicit goods. Thousands allow themselves to be sealed into containers and shipped across the ocean. Rare Indonesian and Brazilian parakeets are smuggled out of jungles by the hundreds. Rogue militarists trade in Russian nuclear materials. Mohawks smuggle contraband tobacco into Canada. TV crews smuggle Saddam and Uday's rare Iraqi paintings. In northern Canada turtles and frogs are smuggled in family sedans, shipped live in crates as cargo around the world. CFCs are strapped on the back of smugglers crossing the Mexican border. In Brazil twelve million animals a year are smuggled for collections or traditional medicines. Two million children a year are smuggled across borders. In Nigeria children are smuggled as 'foodstuffs' and sold to harvest cocoa. Cocaine is smuggled in a leg cast. Arms are smuggled through Syria. A woman smuggles cocaine into a prison in a bible. In the Warsaw Ghetto, food was smuggled in through walls, gates, underground tunnels and sewers. In the 1800s it was gypsum smuggled out of Nova Scotia and New Brunswick. There is always something hidden. There is always someone willing. There is always a shadow to slip through.

Ablation zone

The glacier is cool in her mind. Meltwater carves vertical channels. The stillest place on earth, the Arctic is a lozenge. The Arctic soothes. On the earth's forehead the ice cap drifts from Alaska to Greenland. Slow agitation. Winds at half the speed of an east-coast hurricane. Conglomerate of ice floes freezing and cracking. So far north there is only south. Compass dials spin. Every movement downhill. Not uniformly frozen, the Arctic. Not icebergs like soap cakes. No Victorian inlets with whales dolphining and men with pipes posing on wooden decks. White on white on white, ice stacked and sighing, cascading and breaking apart; the cap beckons, the cap stirs. The cap is solemn. The cap is unskiable; even the blade of an axe must be warmed or it will splinter like glass. Rubber tires explode. Running leaves a trail of steam. Thoughts pierce, words shimmy. Gaps appear, large and glassy moulins. Ablation, what she carries melts faster than what she acquires. Warming, the tip of her nose a dipstick. Nowhere and nothing to burn.

The lover

He still manages to paint. At least he shows up at dinner with splotches on his pants and cap, though never, she notices, on his face. His shoulders touch his ears and are curved, like wings, she thinks, his head always about to go under. When she stands behind him in the dinner line she wants to put her head between his blades and pull. She is afraid his heart might crack. He keeps busy, the lover. He walks to the bar in town where he has heard they have fights. He plays pool badly, and loses. Afternoons he tosses a baseball, always only at first base. The one he loves has red hair and is firm. He will not have her, and perhaps he knows this already. Still, at midnight he finds her yellow room and slips under the door. He believes in everything about her. But the best thing is how she fits him: how she lies on top of him like a cat in a bowl.

The meat painter

There is a young man who paints meat. He is not discerning, any cut will do. He understands the appeal of blood red. Crimson has historical, painterly significance. There is no question about grades. Investigation of commodification is possible. One has to consider isolation, the quality of the cut. There is no backdrop. Steak is not political. It is best displayed against white. There is nothing alarming. He is not strictly into cows. Pork comes in six-packs. Tenderloins fat as thighs. The meat glistens on the canvas. It is cheap meat. Wal-Mart meat. He has to work fast. Later he freezes it to be served at the opening. No particular statement is attached. It is more appropriate to paint cuts of meat than rubber duckies. What is worrying is the light, how the cuts take on personality, how at odd angles some say they have seen Jesus, how even then it still makes her hunger for a skirt steak and string beans.

The biophiliac

Moss eyes, skullcap of grey, she moves, a chisel on the earth. Distinct tinkle of waterfall when she passes. She kneels on the ground with her pinhole camera. Waterfalls and crystalline caverns appear in the prints she develops in the street, on foam, under glass. She is desert rock and a river of colour. She is lithe and compass. Emulsifier of organic energy. A diviner, she tickles the ears. Oh, for those etiolating youth, gangly in videoed basements. Miracle fish: place her in your palm, she will tell you your past. Pendular. Where she has stepped, forget-me-nots. Penetrant, she peels thin film from your eyes, numbing layer of fat at the waist. She is everywhere at once, clipping. No penny stock, not even bottled water, everything open, thumbs wanting someplace to pin you down.

If I weren't so miserable I should never be happy

All night the rain fell through the open window. She dreamed of orange and yellow salamanders. She heard mushrooms sprouting. She heard the robins before sunrise. Still it rains. Umbrellas appear: now red, now blue, now green, no Burberry in Vermont. She stands on the bridge and is happily miserable watching the river rise. Turbid, yellow, it hits the falls, ducktail of a man who smokes too much. It pounds the bank. She thinks of yesterday when the sun shone. She pruned lilacs. The red mill burned. Iris unfolded. The ladder creaked under her. A duckling peeped. Louise waded in with nets in each hand: a grey and blue butterfly she pushed against the current. She scooped the duckling in a net. It shot through like a feather. The duckling surfaced and peeped. Where was its mother? Louise tried again. The women looked on from the bank in their sun hats. They were busy weeding. The sun shone like sugar. Louise tried again and again the duckling slipped through. It shot like a tadpole for the bank. It zigzagged, a puff of cotton against the current. It willed itself to shadow. It hid under the stubborn roots. She imagined a mink there, or a weasel. Perhaps the dog did too. Standing guard on the bank. Sniffing at the cuffs. The drakes watched from a distance. The mother was nowhere to be seen. A goldfinch lit on a branch, crooked its head and pricked her with its beaded eye. There was a buzz in the syrupy air. Bees tumbled in pink locust. The swallow continued sitting in the nest box. A yellow butterfly swooped and shot upward. Men passed by in trucks, oblivious. The marketplace continued its ticking. Interest rates fell. The chef chopped carrots. She twisted and the ladder tipped underfoot. A thousand babies were born in the second it took her to catch her breath. The mother duck was nowhere to be seen. Louise walked back across the river, nets like wings. The sun shone warm as honey. Later, after she had finished pruning, she heard squawking. She saw a mink slinking along the river's edge. A grackle hopped from branch to branch along the bank. She saw the mother duck chase the mink away, magnetic ducklings in tow. She hoped she had found the lost duckling. There was no telling how many had survived. Now the river is too swift even for ducks. The drakes are on the grass waiting. The mother and ducklings are gone. The mink is gone. Louise and the women are gone. The dog is sleeping. Another thousand babies are born. More than have died. Now people skirt the red mill in windbreakers. She stands on the bridge feeling the river swell under her. Somewhere a man stands up and says the river has peaked. A car drives over the covered bridge, just out of view. Somewhere else a fish is caught. But here the river takes another

swipe at the concrete pillars under her feet. Some-
one in the red mill pours a coffee. Sylvia arranges
her bark. The rain lessens. Robins appear, flashes of
copper on the lawn. She is sure there is no music
here. For a fact, there are no ladies.

THE WAVES, AN UNMAKING

'I have made up thousands of stories; I have filled innumerable notebooks with phrases to be used when I have found the true story, the one story to which all these phrases refer. But I have never yet found that story. And I begin to ask, Are there stories?'

'"Like" and "like" and "like" – but what is the thing that lies beneath the semblance of the thing?'

Virginia Woolf

I am not yet twenty-one. I am to be broken.

1

Even in the beginning I was not here.

2

I have no answer. I hear birds. I see them darting in the air but I know nothing of their flight. Life buffets me. Tongues cut. I am insubstantial. I have no face. My mind wanders. My hands follow. Nothing is firm, nothing is nailed down; I do not see the angles and calculations of the world. Words are blows. I feel rivers flow through me, there is a waterfall at my neck. The night sky echoes in my chest. I am bruised. I will succumb. My arms are gashed. In my bed at night all corners are smoothed. Mornings I am washed ashore with seaweed in my ears and salt on the pillow. I find myself once again with Louis, who has grown rich and bold, but I have moments of hesitation, moments of paralysis. I fly to New York. I buy clothes. I go to the cottage. Animals stalk me. I lounge in a Muskoka drinking chardonnay. The sun burns. I feel uncomfortable on airplanes. I penetrate nothing. My cards are maxed. Even Jinny eludes me. My thoughts are dead ends. Life flows through me, around me. I have never been firm. I ride on the air stream of others. I do not understand women. I cannot recommend. Men are railway cars. Men are not destinations. I have no face. I cannot pinpoint how to enter. My mind is a basin. There is no cool water. All is shallow. Lights burn in the back of my head. There is much to be done about me. I am not what you want. I am not what you dreamed of. I was never who I thought. Never what you needed. Where you try and project there is a blank and the blank is endless.

To follow the curve of the sentence, wherever it might lead, into deserts, under drifts of sand, regardless of lures, of seductions …

To be always becoming, always dangling; to be damp, inexact, always wanting to be closer, more precise; to want to explore *the exactitudes of language, and step firmly upon the well-laid sentences*; to live in a world that abandons the present moment and to want only that; to be in love with the world and have it turn its back; to be a poet of undetermined skill; to have given a piece of oneself and have it flung out; to understand the contemptible nature of self; *to be poor always and unkempt; to be ridiculous* in the Eaton Centre; to have written one whole poem and to have it spurned; to pour all of you into air; to know that all will come before us and none of it for me; to know that time presses in and no one comes closer; to have all desire roundly pummelled out of one's skin; to join the procession of the uncounted; to know that poetry exists even if we do not write it; to cling to one's *credentials, like a man clapping in an empty field*; to see the bottom but never touch it; to dream the top and not strive; to know that you have gone past choosing; to know that you let love die, to carry on anyhow, to embrace and wring every drop of time.

Little animal that I am, sucking my flanks in with fear.

My life an expressway; my life telephone poles, felled and erected, felled and erected, a great procession of uprightness. My life standing outside the motorcade, willing myself to enter the great streets, the *sanded paths of victory driven through the jungle.* My life up and down Yonge Street. My life wavering, *even my thin legs ripple like a stalk in the wind.* My life watching Susan tower and flow. My life craving an edge. My life thick carpets and long-stemmed glasses. My life men in good suits. My life with silk thighs. My life always looking past. My life the clear light of day, a floodlight in all dark corners. My life gilt and crystal. My life dazzle, my body a lantern. My life fire, all consuming, all desire to be singled out. My life having drinks at Scaramouche. My life guiding men home. My life always first at the gate. My life grey and civil. My life choosing patterns. Dizzy in lounges in Yorkville, articulate at Tiffany's. My life paying too much for parking. My life from the outside looking in. My life watching. My life a little dog. My life sucking my flanks in with fear.

I detect a certain effort, an extravagance in his phrase, as if he said 'Look!' but Percival says 'No.'

Every day I dig up. I unbury relics of myself.

I, I, I sign my name everywhere, and everywhere is mine. Still I crave. I will never settle. I will never have enough. There is never enough. There is more to take, always, opportunity bends over. One must be present. One must be subscribed. The tentacles of my desire spread exponentially. I take over. I remake. I circle the globe with my eye. I feel war approach and I work harder. I feel my roots penetrate and command. There are a million ways to profit. There are a million ways to split. Once Jinny kissed me. Women always want. Rhoda wants. I, I, I sign my name everywhere. My hand is out. I wait to inherit my rare fruit, my Turkish rugs, my two cars, my collection of art, my wine cellar and humidor – a quick walk to the park – everything present tense. Why then do I recall Jinny kissing me? Why bother with Bernard and Neville? Susan and Rhoda? The thread breaks. The Dow dips. I bolster myself with maps and waistcoats. I remember archaic words. Who is the real hero? Who has gone furthest? I sign my name and the world unfurls. I am a captain of luxury. Nothing is ever whole. One must parcel. One must divide further. One must find ways to charge fees for the minutest interaction. There is no one who undoes me. I am the one who ties the knot. I am the one who says no. I, I, I sign my name everywhere, and everywhere is mine.

Those are white words.

White words clamber at my heel: eggshell, nougat,
Benjamin Moore. I stand in the gallery with my eyes
closed. White screens. Wax. Swimming in milk. I
think of the chalk I hid in the folds of my skirt.
Clouds tumble overhead. They have tails. Someone
is pulling them. I wear linen. I feel bleached, sun-
dried, tart. I smell of lilies. A husband appears. Faces
and more faces. Blanks filling themselves in. I
remember a kiss in a garden. It hangs there. Some-
times I visit it. It pulses. It's hard and purple now. It
spirals in the garden; it flicks its tail. Babies appear
like roots. They trip me up. I move with the pack into
the city. The city is futile. Words tumble. The gallery
is brightly lit. The walls are blank. Possibly there is
no show. Someone shimmers, a blank screen before
me. All of Toronto is sleeping, silent as trumpeter
swans. I alone illuminate and pulse. My mind is a
field. I erect my children like fence posts. I have
given up exteriors. All is indoors for me. I hear waves
breaking. Small lake waves. I pour flour into a mixing
bowl. The antiquated gesture. Everyone is thinking
of Percival. Somewhere my husband is on a train,
shaving. My feet grow cold. I shop underground. I
remember the sand shifting between my toes. Notes
lift into the air. White and fluffy they hit my temples
and ring out. I am sure everyone understands how
my head rings. I am sure everyone knows how dry my
hands are. I am sure everyone can hear white as it

clamours inside my head. Music lifts through the air. It pings and is horsehair on snare; is a tin can and chimes. Now a stick hits on something hard, now click of tongue, now something hollow. The music builds and builds. I stand at the glove counter in Holt Renfrew aware of myself in wool. The stick hits, the pinging repeats and now the horsehair on snare is white in my mind.

Have I read the little gesture of your left hand correctly?

In the beginning, there were waves. The sun was a diamond: every slant and mood a specific shade. *Every hour something new is unburied in the great bran pie.* The waves broke over Neville and Louis and I. They lapped up from the lakeshore. Our skin was tough as birch bark and soft as butterfly wings. We floated. We plunged. We heard the bubble of springs underground. We swore we would find diamonds in granite. In the beginning our movements were erratic, original. We leapt over milkweed, we chased dragonflies, we found ourselves under pine trees; we caught monarchs with our bare hands. I felt in me lava flow, ancient. It needed to burst, to break the surface or harden. Wasn't the tree Atwood's? Hadn't we named them? Were we anything more than feelings? Was anything solid? Neville had a fin on his back. He read Virgil, and later bp and Dewdney, he recognized Ondaatje in the architecture. He surfaced and dove. His scales caught the light. When he flashed, he blinded me. Susan and Rhoda were there, Jinny too. Their fins were dull. They swam slower. Their eyes were disapproving. They pierced. Now I see we swim in shoals. Everything is unfinished. We move into rooms. We leave nature in childhood. We are content to give up air. Our potential opens and closes like coral, it breathes and hardens. We spin lines and hang together, the filament thins, tugs wear. We are vulnerable to weather. Once I loved him. A chair flew across the room. My cigarette spiralled through the air. Later, lights began to dim. The strands pulling thinner.

Now we relent. We take the streetcar. We turn water into wine. We have dinner parties. We become missiles hurled against the city. We mix with unknown quantities. We covet and dive. We come together and split off. We are never sure who we are without others. We marry. We grope in the dark. We buy a semi-detached and pay taxes. We fight termite ants and the privatization of power. We give birth and resist. We regard our daughters like distant emperors. The strands pull thinner and snap. We spiral like spent cigarettes through the air, like maple keys, food for dew worms. We let drop. We shed. We begin to make statements. Questions fall away. They become hooks that catch us as we float. We try not to cling but we cling harder. I find Neville's credentials in my pocket. I see myself in others. All is unfinished. *My little boat bobs unsteadily upon the chopped and tossing waves.* How did I end up alone? Once there was poetry. There were phrases. I grow weary of phrases. All dissolves and so should phrases. Words crash around me. I never forget the mornings at the lake catching tadpoles. I smell Neville's skin always. I hear Susan and Rhoda chasing Jinny who kissed Louis. Everything burns still. Orange believes.

Orange ends the day. Tossed we are rocks in air, sea, foam breaking. I resist straight lines, resist interiors, resist declarations.

And aren't we all plumb lines? We forget everything. We remember nothing. Sparrows nest in our ears. We argue about Dewdney and Bök, Trudeau and Chrétien. We look south and yawn. We marvel. We understand light. Who was the tree? Was I the tree? We muscle upstream and die, but not before the whirr of birds, the swinging of the baton, the crash of markets and hard drives, a cardinal in the palm. Not before the dance and the walk, the dinner party and raised glass. Not before dipping into Glenn Gould and Joni Mitchell, not before the glorious swinging and bustle. Some search in the dark tombs of King Street, others under spires, still others in the couplet and leaf, but I find myself in others and am content. I will not fling myself at death; no, I die daily and am reborn. I look death in the eye; I take less each day. I will give more. I will feel the tug of the newborn before I loosen my grip, before those who have gone before me have settled. There are hooks in the sky that catch and carry us. There is light and air, there is water; we let go of the strand but it continues. It goes on.

... *The Waves*, an architecture

Him Rhoda go under myself how Jinny
Rhoda go under myself how Jinny Him
go under myself how Jinny Him Rhoda
under myself how Jinny Him Rhoda go
myself how Jinny Him Rhoda go under
how Jinny Him Rhoda go under myself
Jinny Him Rhoda go under myself how

is my with that on are the
my with that on are the is
with that on are the is my
that on are the is my with
on are the is my with that
are the is my with that on
the is my with that on are

the and I of a to in
and I of a to in the
I of a to in the and
of a to in the and I
a to in the and I of
to in the and I of a
in the and I of a to

some our up out her us which
our up out her us which some
up out her us which some our
out her us which some our up
her us which some our up out
us which some our up out her
which some our up out her us

it as not we me have at
as not we me have at it
not we me have at it as
we me have at it as not
me have at it as not we
have at it as not we me
at it not we me have at

...

one like this am for be said
like this am for be said one
this am for be said one like
am for be said one like this
for be said one like this am
be said one like this am for
said one like this am for be

...

...

Acknowledgements

This book is, among other things, a direct response to and engagement with the work of Virginia Woolf, but my reading of her texts was radically altered by other writers, including Lisa Robertson, Anne Carson and Gertrude Stein, as well as by general discussion at the Thirteenth Annual Virginia Woolf Conference at Smith College. The epigraph on page 5 is taken from a letter to Vita Sackville West dated March 26, 1926 (*The Letters of Virginia Woolf*, Vol. 3, ed. Nigel Nicholson and Joanne Trautman, Harcourt Brace Jovanovich, 1978). The quote on page 8 is from *Surfacing* by Margaret Atwood (McClelland and Stewart, 1972). The quote on page 11 is from Gertrude Stein's *The Geographical History of America* (Vintage, 1973). The quote on page 23 is from *The Weather*, Lisa Robertson (New Star, 2001). The quote on page 47, and all subsequent titles in 'Virginia, Vanessa, the strands' are from *Moments of Being* (ed. Jeanne Schulkind, Harcourt, 1985). The poems themselves contain references, phrases and echoes from Woolf's text. The second quote on page 47 is from Gaston Bachelard's *The Poetics of Reverie* (Beacon, 1971). The quote from Gertrude Stein, page 57, and the line 'Yes I have but I am not in which is a pity' on page 59 are from *How To Write* (Dover, 1975). The epigraphs on page 64 and 66 are from *Moments of Being*. 'Or: another way of telling' is composed entirely of text collaged from Virginia Woolf's *To the Lighthouse*. I used both the e-text version and the Everyman edition, 1991. *Sumac Leaves Around a Hole* was an installation by Andy Goldsworthy at Storm King Arts Center, 18 October 1998. 'The wall' includes text from *Wall* (Harry N. Abrams, 2000), by Andy Goldsworthy, introduction by Kenneth Baker. 'A lilac begins to leaf' is a line from 'X Ray' by Arthur Sze, with thanks for the inspiration. 'The Smugglers' is a found poem based on a news article and subsequent Internet search. The title on page 85 is taken from the *The Diary of Virginia Woolf*, Vol. 4 (Penguin, 1983). The quotes on page 89, all poem titles and all subsequent quotes in '*The Waves*, an unmaking' are taken from Virginia Woolf's *The Waves* (Grafton Books, 1988). '… *The Waves*, an architecture' is composed of words appearing most frequently in Woolf's *The Waves*. Thanks to the Virginia Woolf Society for the ongoing development of Woolf on the web. Electronic texts supplied by the Oxford Text Archive. Catalogue available at http://ota.ahds.ac.uk/.

And thanks ...

To Jason Dewinetz and Aaron Peck at Greenboat-house for the finely crafted chapbook of 'Still and Otherwise.' To the editors of *The Walrus, New American Writing, The Malahat Review, nth position* and *How2*, for publishing earlier versions of these poems. To the Dodge Foundation for valuable writing time, the Vermont Studio Center for the space, the artists who shared their table and studios, and to Arthur Sze and Carol Moldaw, for early, encouraging responses. To Alana Wilcox at Coach House Books for her interest and support. To Rachel, Erica and belladonna. To Caroline Bergvall and Mark Hussey for conversation and direction. To Danielle Bobker for everything else. I bow to Erin Mouré, fine poet, editor and inspiration. I bow again ... This book is for my sister France, who revealed to me the secret of light.

About the author

Sina Queyras is the author of *Slip* and *Teethmarks*. Recently she edited *Open Field: 30 Contemporary Canadian Poets*. She lives in Brooklyn.

Typeset in Charlotte and Charlotte Sans and printed
and bound at the Coach House on bpNichol Lane,
2006

Edited for the press by Erin Mouré
Cover image by Sina Queyras

Coach House Books
401 Huron St. on bpNichol Lane
Toronto, Ontario M5S 2G5
Canada

416 979 2217
800 367 6360

mail@chbooks.com
www.chbooks.com